DK READERS is a compelling reading programme for children. The programme is designed in conjunction with leading literacy experts, including Cliff Moon M.Ed., who has spent many years as a teacher and teacher educator specializing in reading. Cliff Moon has written more than 160 books for children and teachers. He is series editor to Collins Big Cat.

Beautiful illustrations and superb full-colour photographs combine with engaging, easy-to-read stories to offer a fresh approach to each subject in the series. Each DK READER is guaranteed to capture a child's interest while developing his or her reading skills, general knowledge, and love of reading.

The five levels of DK READERS are aimed at different reading abilities, enabling you to choose the books that are exactly right for your child:

Pre-level 1: Learning to read
Level 1: Beginning to read
Level 2: Beginning to read alone
Level 3: Reading alone
Level 4: Proficient readers

The "normal" age at which a child begins to read can be anywhere from three to eight years old. Adult participation through the lower levels is very helpful for providing encouragement, discussing storylines and sounding out unfamiliar words.

No matter which level you select, you can be sure that you are helping your child learn to read, then read to learn!

LONDON, NEW YORK, MUNICH,
MELBOURNE, and DELHI

Series Editor Deborah Lock
Designer Rosie Levine
Production Editor Sean Daly
Picture Researcher Rob Nunn
Jacket Designer Natalie Godwin

Reading Consultant
Cliff Moon, M.Ed.

Dorling Kindersley Limited
80 Strand, London WC2R 0RL

A CIP catalogue record for this book
is available from the British Library

ISBN: 978-1-40537-637-2

Printed and bound in China by L Rex Printing Co., Ltd.

The publisher would like to thank the following for their kind
permission to reproduce their photographs:
a=above, b=below/bottom, c=centre, l=left, r=right, t=top

Alamy Images: D. Hurst 18fbr; Nikreates 19bc, 31br; Pegaz 20-21.
Corbis: Heide Benser 26-27; Randy Faris 4; Move Art Management
5. **Getty Images:** Fuse 10t; The Image Bank / John Kelly 19t; The
Image Bank / Martin Poole 16t; Lifesize / Yellow Dog Productions
18c, 32clb; Stockbyte / Steve Wisbauer 18br.

All other images © Dorling Kindersley
For further information see www.dkimages.com

Discover more at
www.dk.com

Contents

4   Good morning!

6   Clothes

8   Breakfast

10 Shoes

12 Shapes

14 Games

16 Lunch

18 Playground

20 Music

22 Toys

24 Cooking

26 Bathtime

28 Pyjamas

30 Goodnight!

32 Glossary

DK READERS

LEARNING
pre-level 1
TO READ

My Day

DK

A Dorling Kindersley Book

Good morning!
I wake up and stretch.

arm

It's the start
of a new day.

I wash my face
and put my
clothes on.

T-shirt

 clothes

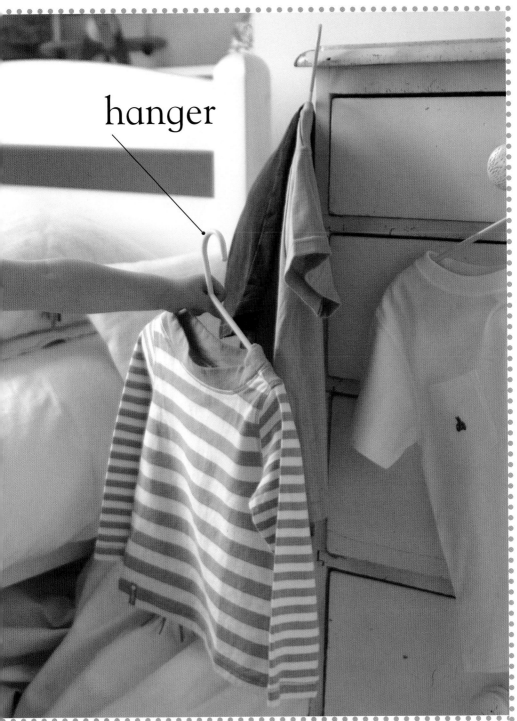

hanger

 breakfast

I have my breakfast.

cereal

bowl

trainers

shoes

I put my shoes and
coat on to go
to school.

coat

I play with the shapes at school.

shapes

square

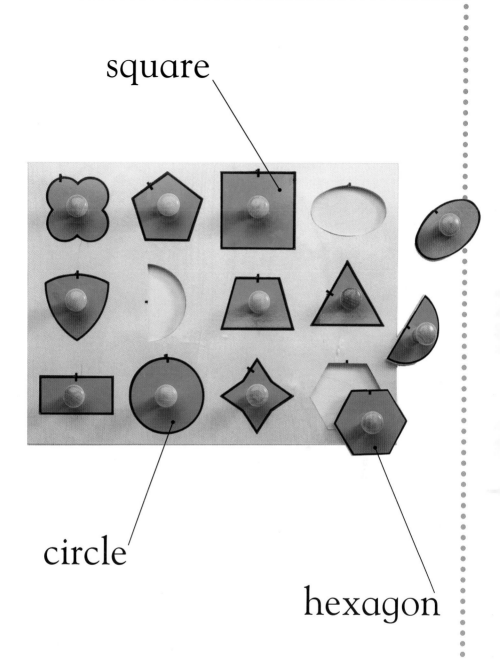

circle

hexagon

 games

I play games
with my class.

It's lunchtime!

apple

water

I have my lunch.

 lunch

tricycle

playground

I play in the playground.

Good afternoon!

music

I dance to music
before I go home.

I play with my toys
when I get home.

train

doll

ball

 toys

peas

cooking

24

rice

I help
to cook tea.

I have a bath and
brush my teeth after
I've eaten my tea.

bathrobe

bathtime

toothbrush

book

 pyjamas

I put my pyjamas on
and then read a book.

teddy bear

I get into bed.
It's the end of my day.

 What did you like

Goodnight!

doing today?

Glossary

 **Breakfast**
is the first meal
of the day.

 **Cook**
is to make food
ready for eating.

 **Lunch**
is a meal eaten in
the middle of the day.

 **Playground**
is an outdoor place
where children play.

 **School**
is a building where
children go to learn.